Big Machines At Work

Forklifts

By Jean Eick

The Child's World® Inc. ◆ Eden Prairie, Minnesota

Published by The Child's World®, Inc.
7081 W. 192 Ave.
Eden Prairie, MN 55346

Copyright © 1999 by the Child's World®, Inc.
All rights reserved. No part of this book may be
reproduced or utilized in any form or by any means
without written permission from the publisher.
Printed in the United States of America.

Design and Production:
The Creative Spark, San Juan Capistrano, CA.

Photos: © 1998 David M. Budd Photography

Library of Congress Cataloging-in-Publication Data
Eick, Jean, 1947-
        Fork lifts at work / by Jean Eick.
            p. cm.
        Includes index.
        Summary: Describes how a fork lift works and how it is used to move heavy loads.
        ISBN 1-56766-530-6 (library reinforced : alk. paper)
        1. Fork lift trucks--Juvenile literature. [1. Fork lift trucks.] I. Title.
    TL296.E37 1998
    621.8'63--dc21   98-3131
                                                                        CIP
                                                                         AC

Contents

On the Job

On the job, forklifts work in lumberyards and warehouses. They stack and unstack heavy loads.

The front of the forklift goes up and down like an elevator. It has two forks, called **lifting prongs**, that can lift heavy loads. The part of the forklift that lifts the prongs up and down is called the **mast**.

Up, up goes the front of the forklift. Its

lifting prongs line up with a heavy load

of lumber that the forklift will lift and

load onto a truck.

When the forks are in front of the load, the forklift moves forward. The lifting prongs slide right under the stack of lumber.

Slowly, the forks lift up the lumber.

Then, the lifting prongs tilt up. This

keeps the heavy load from falling off.

Beep, beep! The forklift backs up.

Down, down comes the heavy load
of lumber.

The forklift slowly backs up

toward the truck waiting for the

lumber. Then it turns around.

15

Now the forklift lifts the lumber

again and puts them on the truck.

18

Beep, beep! The forklift is ready

for another load!

Climb Aboard!

Would you like to sit in the driver's seat? Climb aboard! The forklift's driver is called the **operator**. The operator uses **levers** to control the forklift. Chains pull the lifting prongs up on the mast. When the forklift carries a big load, the operator must back up to see where the forklift is going!

That is because the load blocks the

driver's forward view.

Up Close

1. The operator's seat

2. The chains

3. The lifting prongs

4. The levers

5. The mast

Glossary

levers (LEV-ers)
A forklift's levers are sticks with round knobs on the end. The operator uses them to control the forklift.

lifting prongs (LIFF-ting prongs)
Lifting prongs are the two forks that go up and down on the front of the forklift.

mast (MAST)
The mast is the front part of the forklift that pulls the forks up and down.

operator (OP-er-ay-ter)
The operator is the person who drives the forklift and makes it work.